ACT
NOW

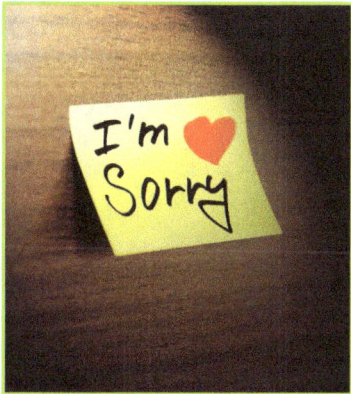

A single misunderstanding, quarrel, or infraction could save or end whatever relationship is at stake, be it personal or business. So, make a difference and extend your sincerest apology by sharing this book, which says "I'm Sorry!" in over 100 languages.

We can create a customized copy for you, where we:

1) Put a reference to you on the front and back covers, or make you the co-author, and
2) Put a letter from you that replaces this page.

We can't imagine a better way for you to say "I'm Sorry!" Can you?

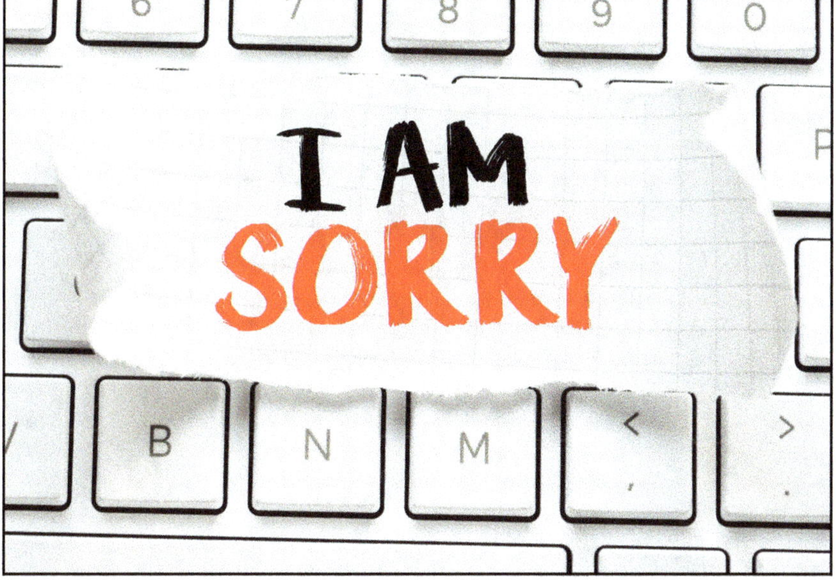
I AM
SORRY

I'm Sorry!

Saying "I'm Sorry!" in More Than 100 Languages

THiNKaha®

E-mail: info@thinkaha.com
20660 Stevens Creek Blvd., Suite 210
Cupertino, CA 95014

Published by THiNKaha®
20660 Stevens Creek Blvd., Suite 210, Cupertino, CA 95014
http://thinkaha.com
E-mail: info@thinkaha.com

First Printing: July 2017
Hardcover ISBN: 978-1-61699-223-1 (1-61699-223-9)
Paperback ISBN: 978-1-61699-222-4 (1-61699-222-0)
eBook ISBN: 978-1-61699-221-7 (1-61699-221-2)
Place of Publication: Silicon Valley, California, USA
Paperback Library of Congress Number: 2017945330

Trademarks

All terms mentioned in this book that are known to be trademarks or service marks have been appropriately capitalized. Neither THiNKaha, nor any of its imprints, can attest to the accuracy of this information. Use of a term in this book should not be regarded as affecting the validity of any trademark or service mark.

Warning and Disclaimer

Every effort has been made to make this book as complete and as accurate as possible. The information provided is on an "as is" basis. The author(s), publisher, and their agents assume no responsibility for errors or omissions. Nor do they assume liability or responsibility to any person or entity with respect to any loss or damages arising from the use of information contained herein.

Sometimes, the best thing you can do is say two simple words. "I'm Sorry!" said authentically is the best way to deal with many situations.

1

More than 100 Languages to say "I'm Sorry!"
http://aha.pub/ImSorry

_____

_____

_____

2

I'm Sorry! (in English) – in more than 100 languages http://aha.pub/ImSorry

_____

_____

_____

3

Aš atsiprašau! (I'm Sorry! in Lithuanian) –
in more than 100 languages
http://aha.pub/ImSorry

_____

_____

_____

4

میں معافی چاہتا ہوں! (I'm Sorry! in Urdu) –
in more than 100 languages
http://aha.pub/ImSorry

_____

_____

_____

5

Συγγνώμη! (I'm Sorry! in Greek) – in more than 100 languages http://aha.pub/ImSorry

_____

_____

_____

6

என்னை மன்னிக்கவம்! (I'm Sorry! in Tamil) – in more than 100 languages
http://aha.pub/ImSorry

_____

_____

_____

7

Przepraszam! (I'm Sorry! in Polish) -
in more than 100 languages
http://aha.pub/ImSorry

8

對不起！(I'm Sorry! in Chinese) -
in more than 100 languages
http://aha.pub/ImSorry

9

Ndiyaxolisa! (I'm Sorry! in Xhosa) – in more than 100 languages http://aha.pub/ImSorry

_____

_____

_____

10

ごめんなさい！(I'm Sorry! in Japanese) –
in more than 100 languages
http://aha.pub/ImSorry

_____

_____

_____

11

JA Prabač! (I'm Sorry! in Belarusian) –
in more than 100 languages
http://aha.pub/ImSorry

_____

_____

_____

12

Jag är ledsen! (I'm Sorry! in Swedish) –
in more than 100 languages
http://aha.pub/ImSorry

_____

_____

_____

13

ខ្ញុំសុំទោស ! (I'm Sorry! in Khmer) – in more
than 100 languages http://aha.pub/ImSorry

_____

_____

_____

14

Žao mi je! (I'm Sorry! in Bosnian) – in more than 100 languages http://aha.pub/ImSorry

_____

_____

_____

15

എന്നോട് ക്ഷമിക്കൂ! (I'm Sorry! in Malayalam) – in more than 100 languages http://aha.pub/ImSorry

_____

_____

_____

16

Ho sento! (I'm Sorry! in Catalan) – in more than 100 languages http://aha.pub/ImSorry

_____

_____

_____

17

मुझे माफ कर दो! (I'm Sorry! in Hindi) –
in more than 100 languages
http://aha.pub/ImSorry

_____

_____

_____

18

Pasayloa ko! (I'm Sorry! in Cebuano) –
in more than 100 languages
http://aha.pub/ImSorry

_____

_____

_____

19

Ndine wachisoni! (I'm Sorry! in Chichewa) –
in more than 100 languages
http://aha.pub/ImSorry

_____

_____

_____

20

Tôi xin lôi! (I'm Sorry! in Vietnamese) –
in more than 100 languages
http://aha.pub/ImSorry

_____

_____

_____

21

Duìbùqǐ! (I'm Sorry! in Chinese) –
in more than 100 languages
http://aha.pub/ImSorry

_____

_____

_____

22

Mi dispiace! (I'm Sorry! in Corsican) –
in more than 100 languages
http://aha.pub/ImSorry

_____

_____

_____

23

ਮੈਨੂੰ ਮੁਆਫ ਕਰੋ! (I'm Sorry! in Punjabi) –
in more than 100 languages
http://aha.pub/ImSorry

_____

_____

_____

24

Üzgünüm! (I'm Sorry! in Turkish) –
in more than 100 languages
http://aha.pub/ImSorry

_____

_____

_____

25

Undskyld! (I'm Sorry! in Danish) – in more
than 100 languages http://aha.pub/ImSorry

_____

_____

_____

26

Het spijt me! (I'm Sorry! in Dutch) –
in more than 100 languages
http://aha.pub/ImSorry

27

Maafkan saya! (I'm Sorry! in Indonesian) –
in more than 100 languages
http://aha.pub/ImSorry

28

Mul on kahju! (I'm Sorry! in Estonian) –
in more than 100 languages
http://aha.pub/ImSorry

29

Ako ay humihingi ng paumanhin!
(I'm Sorry! in Filipino) – in more than 100
languages http://aha.pub/ImSorry

30

Olen pahoillani! (I'm Sorry! in Finnish) –
in more than 100 languages
http://aha.pub/ImSorry

_____

_____

_____

31

Ke kopa tšoarelo! (I'm Sorry! in Sesotho) –
in more than 100 languages
http://aha.pub/ImSorry

_____

_____

_____

32

It spyt my! (I'm Sorry! in Frisian) –
in more than 100 languages
http://aha.pub/ImSorry

_____

_____

_____

33

Síntoo! (I'm Sorry! in Galician) – in more than 100 languages http://aha.pub/ImSorry

_____

_____

_____

34

ვწუხვარ! (I'm Sorry! in Georgian) –
in more than 100 languages
http://aha.pub/ImSorry

_____

_____

_____

35

Bağışlayın! (I'm Sorry! in Azerbaijani) –
in more than 100 languages
http://aha.pub/ImSorry

_____

_____

_____

36

Es tut mir Leid! (I'm Sorry! in German) – in more than 100 languages
http://aha.pub/ImSorry

_____

_____

_____

37

አዝናለሁ! (I'm Sorry! in Amharic) – in more than 100 languages http://aha.pub/ImSorry

_____

_____

_____

38

Syngnómi! (I'm Sorry! in Greek) – in more than 100 languages http://aha.pub/ImSorry

_____

_____

_____

39

Uzr so'rayman! (I'm Sorry! in Uzbek) –
in more than 100 languages
http://aha.pub/ImSorry

_____

_____

_____

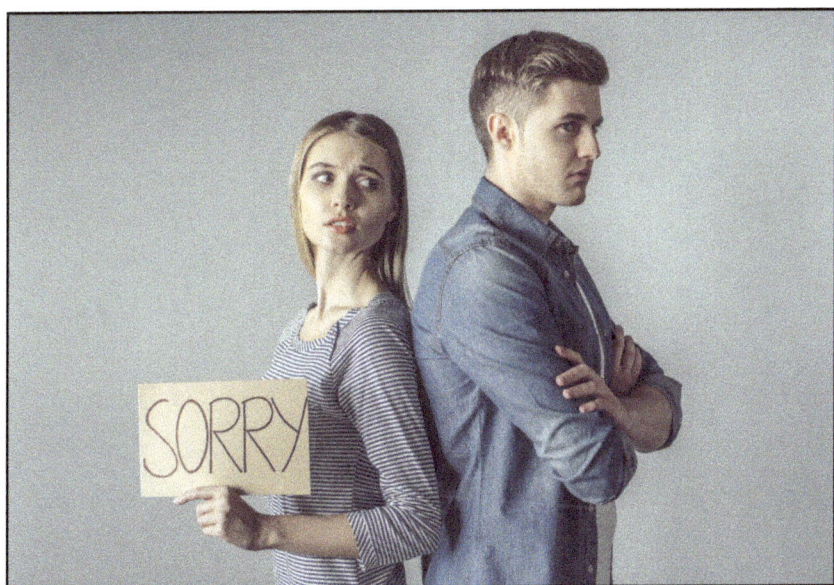

40

હું દિલગીર છું! (I'm Sorry! in Gujarati) –
in more than 100 languages
http://aha.pub/ImSorry

_____

_____

_____

41

Mwen dezole! (I'm Sorry! in Haitian Creole) –
in more than 100 languages
http://aha.pub/ImSorry

_____

_____

_____

42

Au Aroha ahau! (I'm Sorry! in Maori) –
in more than 100 languages
http://aha.pub/ImSorry

_____

_____

_____

43

E kala mai ia'u! (I'm Sorry! in Hawaiian) –
in more than 100 languages
http://aha.pub/ImSorry

44

אנ' מצטער! (I'm Sorry! in Hebrew) –
in more than 100 languages
http://aha.pub/ImSorry

45

Я Прабач! (I'm Sorry! in Belarusian) –
in more than 100 languages
http://aha.pub/ImSorry

_____

_____

46

mujhe maaph kar do! (I'm Sorry!
in Hindi) – in more than 100 languages
http://aha.pub/ImSorry

_____

_____

_____

47

Kuv Thov txim! (I'm Sorry! in Hmong) -
in more than 100 languages
http://aha.pub/ImSorry

_____

_____

_____

48

Sajnálom! (I'm Sorry! in Hungarian) -
in more than 100 languages
http://aha.pub/ImSorry

_____

_____

_____

49

Ma binu! (I'm Sorry! in Yoruba) – in more than 100 languages http://aha.pub/ImSorry

_____

_____

_____

50

Ọ dị m nwute! (I'm Sorry! in Igbo) – in more than 100 languages http://aha.pub/ImSorry

_____

_____

_____

51

Կներես! (I'm Sorry! in Armenian) – in more than 100 languages http://aha.pub/ImSorry

_____

_____

_____

52

මට සමාවෙන්න! (I'm Sorry! in Sinhala) –
in more than 100 languages
http://aha.pub/ImSorry

_____

_____

_____

53

Mi dispiace! (I'm Sorry! in Italian) –
in more than 100 languages
http://aha.pub/ImSorry

_____

_____

_____

54

Sŭzhalyavam! (I'm Sorry! in Bulgarian) –
in more than 100 languages
http://aha.pub/ImSorry

_____

_____

_____

55

Aku Sorry! (I'm Sorry! in Javanese) –
in more than 100 languages
http://aha.pub/ImSorry

56

ನನ್ನನ್ನು ಕ್ಷಮಿಸು! (I'm Sorry! in Kannada) –
in more than 100 languages
http://aha.pub/ImSorry

57

Mi bedaŭras! (I'm Sorry! in Esperanto) –
in more than 100 languages
http://aha.pub/ImSorry

_____

_____

_____

58

Keşiriñiz! (I'm Sorry! in Kazakh) –
in more than 100 languages
http://aha.pub/ImSorry

59

Omlouvám se! (I'm Sorry! in Czech) –
in more than 100 languages
http://aha.pub/ImSorry

60

khnhom somtosa! (I'm Sorry! in Khmer) –
in more than 100 languages
http://aha.pub/ImSorry

_____

_____

_____

61

¡Lo siento! (I'm Sorry! in Spanish) –
in more than 100 languages
http://aha.pub/ImSorry

62

joesong haeyo! (I'm Sorry! in Korean) –
in more than 100 languages
http://aha.pub/ImSorry

63

Bibûre! (I'm Sorry! in Kurdish) – in more than 100 languages http://aha.pub/ImSorry

_____

_____

_____

64

Кечирим сурайм! (I'm Sorry! in Kyrgyz) –
in more than 100 languages
http://aha.pub/ImSorry

65

ຂ້ອຍຂໍໂທດ! (I'm Sorry! in Lao) –
in more than 100 languages
http://aha.pub/ImSorry

66

Ego paenitet! (I'm Sorry! in Latin) – in more than 100 languages http://aha.pub/ImSorry

_____

_____

_____

67

Man žēl! (I'm Sorry! in Latvian) – in more than 100 languages http://aha.pub/ImSorry

_____

_____

_____

68

Ek is jammer! (I'm Sorry! in Afrikaans) –
in more than 100 languages
http://aha.pub/ImSorry

_____

_____

_____

69

Et deet mir Leed! (I'm Sorry! in
Luxembourgish) – in more than 100
languages http://aha.pub/ImSorry

_____

_____

_____

70

Жал ми е! (I'm Sorry! in Macedonian) –
in more than 100 languages
http://aha.pub/ImSorry

_____

_____

_____

71

Je suis désolé! (I'm Sorry! in French) –
in more than 100 languages
http://aha.pub/ImSorry

_____

_____

_____

72

Miala tsiny aho! (I'm Sorry! in Malagasy) – in more than 100 languages
http://aha.pub/ImSorry

_____

_____

_____

73

Saya minta maaf! (I'm Sorry! in Malay) –
in more than 100 languages
http://aha.pub/ImSorry

_____

_____

_____

74

Na tuba! (I'm Sorry! in Hausa) –
in more than 100 languages
http://aha.pub/ImSorry

75

Jiddispjaċini! (I'm Sorry! in Maltese) –
in more than 100 languages
http://aha.pub/ImSorry

76

أنا آسف! (I'm Sorry! in Arabic) – in more than 100 languages http://aha.pub/ImSorry

_____

_____

_____

77

मला माफ करा! (I'm Sorry! in Marathi) –
in more than 100 languages
http://aha.pub/ImSorry

_____

_____

_____

78

Barkatu! (I'm Sorry! in Basque) –
in more than 100 languages
http://aha.pub/ImSorry

_____

_____

_____

79

Намайг уучлаарай! (I'm Sorry! in Mongolian) – in more than 100 languages
http://aha.pub/ImSorry

_____

_____

_____

80

ko hcatemakaunggparbhuu! (I'm Sorry! in Burmese) – in more than 100 languages http://aha.pub/ImSorry

_____

_____

_____

81

मलाई माफ गरदिउ! (I'm Sorry! in Nepali) – in more than 100 languages http://aha.pub/ImSorry

_____

_____

_____

82

Ngiyaxolisa! (I'm Sorry! in Zulu) –
in more than 100 languages
http://aha.pub/ImSorry

_____

_____

_____

83

Unnskyld! (I'm Sorry! in Norwegian) –
in more than 100 languages
http://aha.pub/ImSorry

_____

_____

_____

84

زه بخښنه غواړم! (I'm Sorry! in Pashto) – in more than 100 languages
http://aha.pub/ImSorry

_____

_____

85

متاسفم! (I'm Sorry! in Persian) –
in more than 100 languages
http://aha.pub/ImSorry

86

Съжалявам! (I'm Sorry! in Bulgarian) –
in more than 100 languages
http://aha.pub/ImSorry

87

Eu sinto Muito! (I'm Sorry! in Portuguese) – in more than 100 languages
http://aha.pub/ImSorry

_____

_____

_____

88

Žao mi je! (I'm Sorry! in Croatian) –
in more than 100 languages
http://aha.pub/ImSorry

_____

_____

_____

89

Mainū mu'āpha karō! (I'm Sorry! in Punjabi) –
in more than 100 languages
http://aha.pub/ImSorry

_____

_____

_____

90

Imi pare rau! (I'm Sorry! in Romanian) –
in more than 100 languages
http://aha.pub/ImSorry

_____

_____

_____

91

Прости! (I'm Sorry! in Russian) –
in more than 100 languages
http://aha.pub/ImSorry

92

Ua ou faanoanoa! (I'm Sorry! in Samoan) –
in more than 100 languages
http://aha.pub/ImSorry

93

Tha mi duilich! (I'm Sorry! in Scots Gaelic) –
in more than 100 languages
http://aha.pub/ImSorry

_____

_____

_____

94

Жао ми је! (I'm Sorry! in Serbian) –
in more than 100 languages
http://aha.pub/ImSorry

95

Кешіріңіз! (I'm Sorry! in Kazakh) –
in more than 100 languages
http://aha.pub/ImSorry

_____

_____

_____

96

Ndine hurombo! (I'm Sorry! in Shona) –
in more than 100 languages
http://aha.pub/ImSorry

_____

_____

_____

97

مونڪي معاف ڪجو! (I'm Sorry! in Sindhi) –
in more than 100 languages
http://aha.pub/ImSorry

_____

_____

_____

98

죄송 해요! (I'm Sorry! in Korean) –
in more than 100 languages
http://aha.pub/ImSorry

_____

_____

_____

99

Prepáč! (I'm Sorry! in Slovak) – in more than 100 languages http://aha.pub/ImSorry

_____

_____

_____

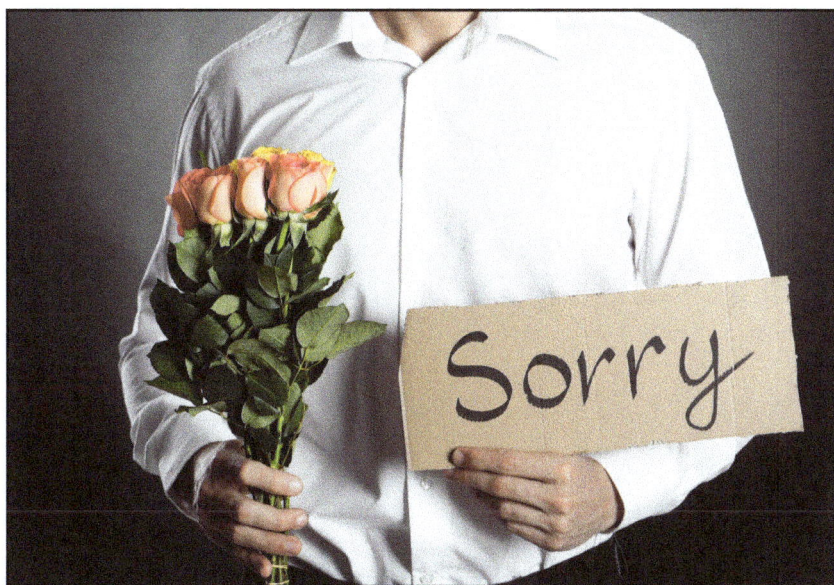

100

Žal mi je! (I'm Sorry! in Slovenian) – in more than 100 languages http://aha.pub/ImSorry

_____

_____

_____

101

Waan ka xumahay! (I'm Sorry! in Somali) –
in more than 100 languages
http://aha.pub/ImSorry

_____

_____

_____

102

Tá brón orm! (I'm Sorry! in Irish) –
in more than 100 languages
http://aha.pub/ImSorry

_____

_____

_____

103

Abdi nyungkeun hapunten! (I'm Sorry! in Sundanese) – in more than 100 languages
http://aha.pub/ImSorry

_____

_____

_____

104

Samahani! (I'm Sorry! in Swahili) –
in more than 100 languages
http://aha.pub/ImSorry

_____

_____

_____

105

Žal mi e! (I'm Sorry! in Macedonian) –
in more than 100 languages
http://aha.pub/ImSorry

_____

_____

_____

106

Мебахшй! (I'm Sorry! in Tajik) – in more than 100 languages http://aha.pub/ImSorry

_____

_____

_____

107

আমি দুঃখিত! (I'm Sorry! in Bengali) –
in more than 100 languages
http://aha.pub/ImSorry

_____

_____

_____

108

నన్ను క్షమించండి! (I'm Sorry! in Telugu) –
in more than 100 languages
http://aha.pub/ImSorry

_____

_____

_____

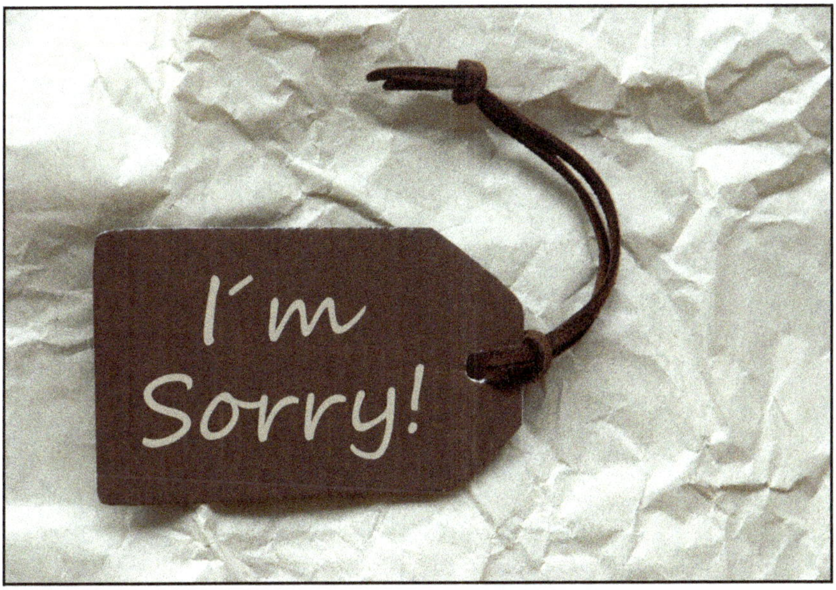
I´m
Sorry!

109

ฉันขอโทษ! (I'm Sorry! in Thai) – in
more than 100 languages
http://aha.pub/ImSorry

_____

_____

_____

110

Huṁ dilagīra chuṁ! (I'm Sorry! in
Gujarati) – in more than 100 languages
http://aha.pub/ImSorry

_____

_____

_____

111

Я Вибач! (I'm Sorry! in Ukrainian) –
in more than 100 languages
http://aha.pub/ImSorry

_____

_____

_____

112

Më vjen keq! (I'm Sorry! in Albanian) –
in more than 100 languages
http://aha.pub/ImSorry

_____

_____

_____

113

Fyrirgefðu! (I'm Sorry! in Icelandic) –
in more than 100 languages
http://aha.pub/ImSorry

_____

_____

_____

114

vtsukhvar! (I'm Sorry! in Georgian) – in more than 100 languages
http://aha.pub/ImSorry

_____

_____

_____

115

Mae'n ddrwg gen i! (I'm Sorry! in Welsh) -
in more than 100 languages
http://aha.pub/ImSorry

_____

_____

_____

116

Āmi duḥkhita! (I'm Sorry! in Bengali) -
in more than 100 languages
http://aha.pub/ImSorry

_____

_____

_____

117

אנטשולדיגט! (I'm Sorry! in Yiddish) –
in more than 100 languages
http://aha.pub/ImSorry

_____

_____

118

Malā māpha karā! (I'm Sorry! in Marathi) –
in more than 100 languages
http://aha.pub/ImSorry

_____

_____

_____

119

Malā'ī māpha garidē'u! (I'm Sorry!
in Nepali) – in more than 100 languages
http://aha.pub/ImSorry

_____

_____

_____

AHAthat™

AHAthat makes it easy to share, author, and promote content. There are over 40,000 quotes (AHAmessages™) by thought leaders from around the world that you can share in seconds for free.

For those who want to author their own book, we have time-tested proven processes that allow you to write your AHAbook™ of 140 digestible, bite-sized morsels in eight hours or less. Once your content is on AHAthat, you have a customized link that you can use to have your fans/advocates share your content and help grow your network.

➲ Start sharing: http://AHAthat.com

➲ Start authoring: http://AHAthat.com/Author

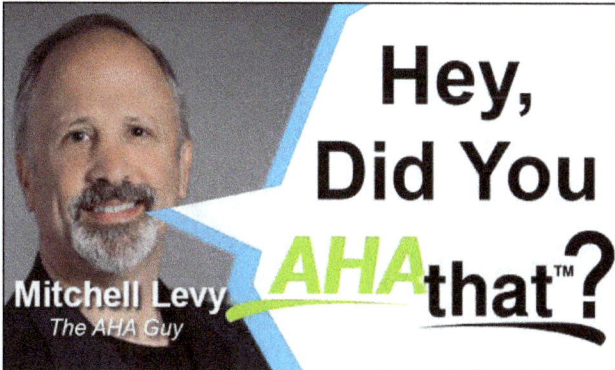

Please go directly to this book in AHAthat and share each AHAmessage socially at http://aha.pub/ImSorry.

Own a Phrase,
Make It Your Own!

Is there a phrase that you're known for or want to be known for? Want us to create a social media-enabled eBook and physical book for you with that phrase in 100+ languages?

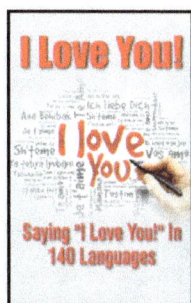

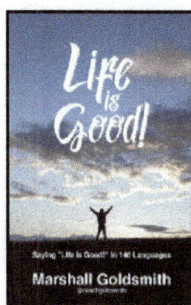

www.ingramcontent.com/pod-product-compliance
Lightning Source LLC
LaVergne TN
LVHW021134080426
835509LV00010B/1352